*Countries Around the World*

# Germany

Mary Colson

Heinemann Library
Chicago, Illinois

**www.heinemannraintree.com**
Visit our website to find out more information about Heinemann-Raintree books.

**To order:**
☎ Phone 888-454-2279
💻 Visit www.heinemannraintree.com to browse our catalog and order online.

© 2012 Heinemann Library
an imprint of Capstone Global Library, LLC
Chicago, Illinois

Edited by Louise Galpine, Kate DeVilliers, and Laura Knowles
Designed by Richard Parker
Original illustrations © Capstone Global Library Ltd 2011
Illustrated by Oxford Designers & Illustrators
Picture research by Liz Alexander
Originated by Capstone Global Library Ltd
Printed in China by CTPS

15 14 13 12 11
10 9 8 7 6 5 4 3 2 1

Library of Congress Cataloging-in-Publication Data
Colson, Mary.
  Germany / Mary Colson.
    p. cm.—(Countries around the world)
  Includes bibliographical references and index.
  ISBN 978-1-4329-5204-4 (hc)—ISBN 978-1-4329-5229-7 (pb)  1.
Germany—Juvenile literature.  I. Title.
  DD17.C655 2012
  943—dc22
                            2010044772

**Acknowledgments**
We would like to thank the following for permission to reproduce photographs: Alamy pp. 7 (© North Wind Picture Archives), 10 (© World History Archive), 11 (© F1online digitale Bildagentur GmbH), 17 (© imagebroker), 27 (© imagebroker), 29 (© Ray Roberts); Corbis pp. 9 (© Bettmann), 12 (© Bettmann), 37 (© Klaus-Dietmar Gabbert/epa); Getty Images pp. 6 (SuperStock), 13 (Tom Stoddart), 21 (Thorsten Rother), 31 (Peter Wafzig); iStockphoto pp. 23 (© rotofrank), 5 (© Arto Hakola), 19 (© riekephotos), 20 (© Kaido Karner), 24 (© Markus Gann), 32 (© Jakub Cejpek), 34 (© Losevsky Pavel), 35 (© HLPhoto), 46 (© Route66).

Cover photograph of a Ferris wheel at Oktoberfest, Munich, Germany, reproduced with permission of Corbis/© RelaXimages.

We would like to thank Rob Bowden for his invaluable help in the preparation of this book.

Every effort has been made to contact copyright holders of material reproduced in this book. Any omissions will be rectified in subsequent printings if notice is given to the publisher.

**Disclaimer**
All the Internet addresses (URLs) given in this book were valid at the time of going to press. However, due to the dynamic nature of the Internet, some addresses may have changed, or sites may have changed or ceased to exist since publication. While the author and publisher regret any inconvenience this may cause readers, no responsibility for any such changes can be accepted by either the author or the publisher.

# Contents

Some words are printed in bold, **like this**. You can find out what they mean by looking in the glossary.

# Introducing Germany

What do you think of when you think of Germany? Do you think of beer and sausages? Or do you think of world wars and the Berlin Wall? Famous for **classical** music, winning soccer World Cups, and trains that run on time, Germany is much more than its **stereotypes**.

Germany's history is full of tragedy and triumph. Today, Germany is a leader in **European Union** politics, and Berlin is the capital of a vibrant modern society with museums, galleries, cafés, and bold architecture at every turn.

## Border control

Germany has been divided, expanded, and reunited more times than most European countries, and it has only been a nation **state** since 1871. The country changed shape again in 1990, making it one of the youngest European countries. It shares borders with nine other countries and lies geographically in the center of Europe. The German flag has three equal horizontal bands of black, red, and gold.

## Global impact

German writers, such as the Brothers Grimm, created fairy tales that have delighted children for generations. German musicians, such as Schumann, Bach, and Beethoven, have composed some of the world's most famous music. German inventors are responsible for the printing press and the rocket engine.

## How to say...

| | | |
|---|---|---|
| **good morning** | *guten morgen* | (gooten moregun) |
| **how are you?** | *wie geht's?* | (vee gates) |
| **I'm fine** | *mir geht's gut* | (meer gates goot) |
| **my name is...** | *Ich heiße...* | (ik highsa) |
| **I come from...** | *Ich komme aus...* | (ik comma ows) |
| **see you later!** | *bis bald!* | (bis balt) |
| **bye!** | *tschuss!* | (choos) |

Germany's dramatic landscape includes emerald lakes and snow-capped mountains, such as these in the Berchtesgaden National Park.

# History: From Warring Tribes to United People

Two thousand years ago, the Romans ruled over an area called Germania. Germania's early settlers were made up of different **tribes**. The Celts, the Vandals, and the Goths fought each other for land and resources. The Vandals were famous for being particularly good warriors.

## The Holy Roman Empire

By the 700s CE, the warring tribes were brought together under one man: Charlemagne (768–814 CE). He ruled over the **Holy Roman Empire**, which included modern-day Germany, France, the Netherlands, and northern Italy.

After Charlemagne's death, the emperors that followed struggled to keep control. The princes and dukes gradually became more powerful in their homelands, and by the 1400s they were independent rulers of their own territories. They created their own laws and controlled their own armies. The **Roman Catholic** Church was also gaining power and influence.

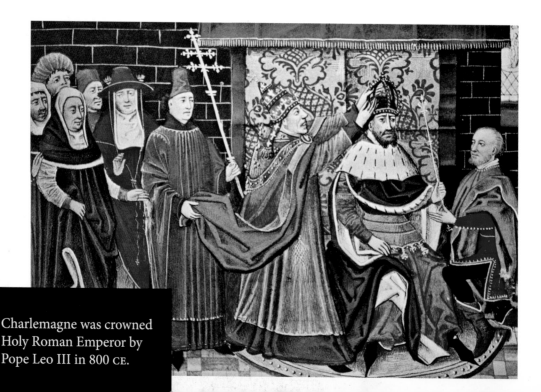

Charlemagne was crowned Holy Roman Emperor by Pope Leo III in 800 CE.

## Wars of religion

By 1517 a growing number of people wanted to change the Church. When a monk named Martin Luther nailed a list of 95 complaints against the Church to the door of the cathedral in Wittenberg, it marked the start of the **Reformation**. After nearly 150 years of devastating religious wars between Catholics and **Protestants** across Europe, the Peace of Westphalia was signed in 1648, and the fighting ended.

### JOHANNES GUTENBERG (c.1400–1468)

Around 1440, Johannes Gutenberg invented the printing press. Books were no longer written slowly by hand, as Gutenberg's press could print dozens of pages a day. Books like the Bible became more easily available. People started to read the Bible and think about its meaning for themselves. This made some people question what the Church was telling them.

In this painting Johannes Gutenberg is demonstrating his printing press.

## After the empire

In 1806, the Holy Roman Empire ended after a failed war against France. From then until 1871, Germany was made up of a patchwork of kingdoms, **dukedoms**, **bishoprics**, and **city states**. German peoples included the Franks, the Saxons, the Hessians, the Bavarians, and the Swabians, each with their own customs and traditions.

## OTTO VON BISMARCK (1815–1898)

Otto von Bismarck was responsible for bringing the German states together into one country. He wanted to create a strong sense of **national identity**. He even started wars with France and Austria to get the German states to unite. After **unification** in 1871, he became the first **chancellor**, or leader, of Germany.

## World War I

By the early 1900s, political tensions over land and borders were growing in Europe. The shooting of the German **noble** Archduke Franz Ferdinand in 1914 sparked a war. Within weeks of his death, German forces invaded Belgium, Luxembourg, and France leading to four years of fighting.

World War I devastated much of Europe, and millions of people lost their lives. British, American, and French forces were just some of those fighting the German army. Eventually, Germany surrendered on November 11, 1918. The world hoped that Germany would never again be able to start a war.

## Between the wars

In the 1920s and 30s, German artistic **culture** flourished. The horrors of war were over, and there was a new freedom of expression. The Bauhaus school of **architecture** created futuristic buildings. Kurt Weill and the Austrian Lotte Lenya wrote and performed popular songs and modern operas. Max Ernst created fantastic dreamlike paintings and sculptures.

Here, German soldiers are fighting in the trenches during World War I.

## Hitler and the rise of Nazism

In 1921 Adolf Hitler became the leader of the National Socialist German Workers (Nazi) Party. His powerful speeches won millions of supporters across Germany. By 1933 Hitler was chancellor.

Hitler made powerful speeches at large rallies and gatherings.

## YOUNG PEOPLE

The Hitler Youth was a **compulsory** club for young people between the ages of 10 and 18. The club leaders tried to turn children into loyal supporters of Hitler and prepared them for military service. In 1936 all other youth organizations were banned.

## The death camps

Hitler blamed Jewish people for many of Germany's problems, and he created laws that reduced their rights. Jews were banned from owning businesses, and they had to wear a yellow star to identify themselves.

In 1939 Germany invaded Poland, and World War II began. By this time many Jews had fled to other countries. Those who stayed were rounded up by the police and sent on trains to **concentration camps**, such as Auschwitz.

There, an estimated six million people, including Jews, gypsies, homeless people, Russians, and political opponents of Hitler, were gassed to death.

Britain, the United States, France, and Russia joined forces to defeat Hitler and stop Nazi Germany from creating an empire. By 1945 German forces were losing the war. Rather than be captured, Adolf Hitler committed suicide, and Germany surrendered.

## SOPHIE SCHOLL (1921-1943)

Not all German people agreed with Hitler and what was happening. Twenty-one-year-old Sophie Scholl was a member of the White Rose Resistance, which urged people to oppose Hitler. In 1943 Sophie and four other members of the group were caught distributing political leaflets. They were arrested, charged with high treason, and executed.

This section of the Jewish Museum in Berlin is in remembrance of the Jewish victims of World War II.

## A wall and a new country

At the end of World War II, Britain, the United States, France, and Russia discussed the best way of keeping Germany peaceful. As a result, Germany was divided in two, creating West Germany and East Germany. West Germany was **democratic**, while East Germany became **communist**. Berlin was also divided into East and West Berlin.

Many people wanted to live in freedom in West Berlin, so they started leaving East Berlin. The communist **authorities** had to do something to stop them.

## The Berlin Wall

In 1961, a high concrete wall was built right through the middle of the city. Thousands of families found themselves on different sides. Some people tried to escape to West Berlin through tunnels or by climbing over the wall. Some succeeded, but many failed and were shot.

The most famous crossing point between East and West Berlin was called Checkpoint Charlie.

## One Germany

In November 1989, huge protests in East Berlin led to the Berlin Wall being torn down, and thousands of people crossed from east to west. The East German communist government collapsed, and so East and West Germany were reunited. German Unity Day is now celebrated on October 3.

In 1989, everybody helped to break down the hated Berlin Wall.

Today, Germany is a **multicultural**, forward-looking country. It is at the heart of European politics, leading debate and finding peaceful solutions.

## YOUNG PEOPLE

On July 21, 1990, rock band Pink Floyd staged a rock concert in Berlin to celebrate the fall of the Berlin Wall. Pink Floyd's album *The Wall* tells the story of a man's isolation from society as he builds a symbolic wall. In the end, he tears the wall down and starts again, just like Berlin and Germany.

# Regions and Resources: Land and Industry

Germany is a land of contrasts and natural beauty. In the north, a great plain of land stretches along the Baltic Sea coast. Gentle hills cover the center of the country leading to the dramatic mountains of the Bavarian Alps in the south. The highest point is the Zugspitze at 9,721 feet (2,963 meters).

## Natural wonders

In the west, the Balver Höhle is Europe's largest cave. It is so large it is used to stage concerts and plays. The Aachtopf in Swabia is Germany's biggest natural spring, producing 2,250 gallons (8,500 liters) of water per second. The mysterious Lorelei rock in the middle of the Rhine soars some 393 feet (120 meters) above the water.

### How to say...

| | | |
|---|---|---|
| **river** | *der Fluss* | (dare floos) |
| **mountain** | *der Berg* | (dare bairg) |
| **lake** | *der See* | (dare zee) |
| **coast** | *die Küste* | (dee koosta) |
| **cave** | *die Höhle* | (dee hurla) |
| **sea** | *das Meer* | (das mere) |
| **forest** | *der Wald* | (dare valt) |
| **valley** | *das Tal* | (das tarl) |

## Neighbors and numbers

Germany covers an area of about 137,846 square miles (357,022 square kilometers) and borders Poland, Denmark, France, the Netherlands, Belgium, Switzerland, Austria, Luxembourg, and the Czech Republic. It has coastline on both the North Sea and the Baltic Sea. Germany's major rivers are the Rhine, the Elbe, the Danube, and the Main. These rivers are used to transport industrial **freight** to the major seaports of Hamburg, Bremen, and Kiel.

This map shows the main landscape features of Germany.

## Weather report

The weather in Germany varies according to region. The Alpine regions have colder winters and cooler summers, but the rest of the country gets very warm, with summer temperatures between 68 and 86° Fahrenheit (20 and 30° Celsius).

Land height:
- Over 1000 meters
- Over 200 meters
- Above sea level
- Below sea level
- Country borders

DENMARK
Baltic Sea
North Sea
Kiel
Hamburg
Bremen
Elbe
THE NETHERLANDS
Berlin ■
POLAND
Balver Höhle
**G E R M A N Y**
Dusseldorf
Cologne
BELGIUM
Rhine
Frankfurt
Main
LUXEMBOURG
CZECH REPUBLIC
FRANCE
N
Danube
Munich
Lake Constance
▲ Zugspitze
SWITZERLAND
AUSTRIA

This chart shows the average monthly rainfall and temperatures in Berlin, Germany's capital.

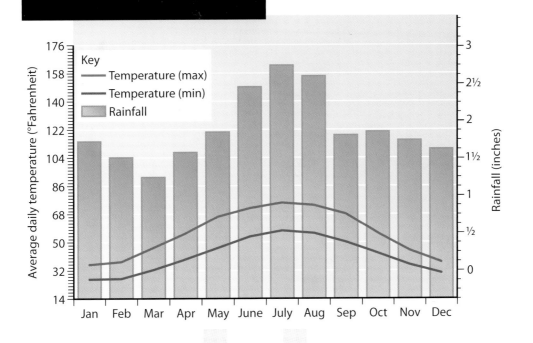

Key
— Temperature (max)
— Temperature (min)
▢ Rainfall

Average daily temperature (°Fahrenheit): 176, 158, 140, 122, 104, 86, 68, 50, 32, 14

Rainfall (inches): 3, 2½, 2, 1½, 1, ½, 0

Jan  Feb  Mar  Apr  May  June  July  Aug  Sep  Oct  Nov  Dec

# Regions of Germany

Germany is divided up into 16 states called *Bundesländer*. Each state has its own coat of arms. Bavaria is the largest state at 27,239 square miles (70,549 square kilometers), but North Rhine-Westphalia has the most people, with 18,075,000.

Key:
— Country borders
— Regional borders

# Industrial nation

North Rhine-Westphalia and the Saarland are Germany's main industrial regions. Cars, light aircraft, and machinery are all made here. Iron and steelworks dot the landscape, too. In the eastern part of the country, Brandenburg and Saxony are the main coal-mining states.

Germany has some of the most modern car factories in the world.

Baden-Württemberg is one of the wealthiest states in Germany, with over a million people employed in mechanical and electrical engineering alone. Daimler and Porsche have large car factories there. The state of Bavaria has one of the largest **economies** in Europe. BMW, Audi, Puma, and Adidas all have factories in the state capital, Munich.

## Agricultural states

Over one million Germans work on the land. Schleswig-Holstein has a large dairy industry, Rhineland-Palatinate is where the German wine industry is based, and the plains of Mecklenburg-West Pomerania are where most food crops are grown.

### Daily life

Each year, nearly a quarter of a million Polish and Romanian seasonal workers arrive in Baden-Württemberg and Lower Saxony to pick white asparagus, or *spargel*. They work up to 12 hours a day, 7 days a week. They earn 5 euros per hour.

## Economic status

Germany has the largest economy in Europe and the fifth largest in the world, worth nearly $3 trillion per year. It is a member of the **G8** richest countries and is in the Eurozone of 16 European countries that use the euro as currency. The euro's symbol is €. Germany has a workforce of over 43 million people, and the average yearly income is $34,100.

## Natural resources

Germany's best natural **resource** is its fertile farmland. Potatoes, wheat, barley, rye, and sugar beet are the main crops. There are some oil, gas, and coal reserves along with copper and iron ore. A third of the country is forest, providing an important timber industry.

Use the key on this map to find out where different natural resources come from in Germany.

Key:
△ Zinc
△ Iron and steel
△ Iron ore
▲ Coal
△ Cement
▲ Gypsum
△ Lead
△ Ferroalloys
△ Aluminum
▲ Lignite
▲ Uranium
△ Sepiolite
△ Potash
⬤ Barite
⬤ Fluorspar
◯ Natural gas
◯ Clays
⬤ Crude petroleum
🌢 Petroleum refinery products

Old mine complexes like this one at Zollverein, near Essen, are now **World Heritage Sites**.

## Trade: buying and selling

Germany's most important **trading** partners are France, the United States, the Netherlands, and Great Britain. Germany **imports** and **exports** machinery, vehicles, chemicals, foodstuffs, textiles, and metals.

The **credit crunch** that began in 2008 caused many job losses in Germany. The richer western half of Germany still supports the poorer eastern half, where unemployment is almost double the national average. Many people leave the former east to find work in the west.

## YOUNG PEOPLE

In Germany, you can start an apprenticeship for a trade, such as plumbing or carpentry, at age 15. This lasts for three years, with four days a week of paid work and one day of schooling. Today, youth **unemployment** is around 10 percent, one of the lowest rates in Europe.

# Wildlife: Protecting the Environment

Germany's rivers, lakes, forests, coasts, and heaths support a wide variety of animals, plants, and **ecosystems**. Many of Germany's native animals are forest-dwelling, such as deer, wild boar, and wolves.

## YOUNG PEOPLE

The Junior Ranger Program enables children who live close to national parks to get involved in protecting them. Children can spend time with rangers, help to take surveys, or map fragile areas. They can also get involved online with the WebRangers.

## Endangered symbol

One of the most vulnerable and now protected animals is the eagle. The white-tailed eagle has been the national symbol of Germany since the Romans ruled Germania. Today strict laws protect its **habitats**.

Conservation work has helped the number of white-tailed eagles in Germany increase in recent years.

The Wadden Sea wetlands are now protected and are an important habitat for sea birds.

## Wetland wonder

The Wadden Sea is an important wetland lying on Germany's North Sea coast. It is home to migratory birds like Arctic terns, but is in danger from pollution. New laws have been passed to clean up the rivers that meet the sea here. Tourists are transported by horse and cart to minimize human impact.

## National parks

Germany's 14 national parks protect an area of more than 3,700 square miles (9,600 square kilometers). From the ancient beech forests of the Eifel and the mudflats of the Wadden Sea, to the eroded rock formations that dominate Saxon Switzerland, the parks protect the country's unique landscapes and wildlife habitats.

### How to say...

| | | |
|---|---|---|
| **rabbit** | *das Kaninchen* | (das kaninshun) |
| **bird** | *der Vogel* | (dare vogle) |
| **bear** | *der Bär* | (dare bare) |
| **boar** | *der Eber* | (dare ayber) |
| **deer** | *das Reh* | (das ray) |
| **eagle** | *der Adler* | dare ardler) |
| **bat** | *der Hieb* | (dare heeb) |
| **falcon** | *der Falke* | (dare falka) |
| **fish** | *der Fisch* | (dare fish) |
| **wolf** | *der Wolf* | (dare vurlf) |

## Being green

Germany is one of the most environmentally aware countries in Europe. Many of the worst environmental problems are in the former East German industrial cities, with polluted rivers and acid rain affecting forests. Strict laws now govern factory **emissions** across the country.

## YOUNG PEOPLE

The annual German National Environment Competition is open to young people between the ages of 13 and 21. Working in groups, teenagers have to investigate an environmental problem and design and implement **sustainable** solutions. If they win, they represent Germany at an international youth environmental conference.

## Eco-targets

Germany has signed on to international treaties on climate change, such as the Kyoto Protocol, which commits countries to reducing greenhouse gas emissions. The government has set a target of cutting emissions by 40 percent by 2020, and 80–85 percent by 2050.

Germany is planning to get all of its electricity from **renewable energy** sources by 2050. It is the world's second largest wind power producer after the United States. In the last ten years, over 300,000 jobs have been created in the renewable energy industry.

## How to say...

| | | |
|---|---|---|
| **environment** | *die Umwelt* | (dee oomvelt) |
| **global warming** | *die globale Erwärmung* | (dee glowbarla airvairmung) |
| **recycling** | *das Recycling* | (das recycling) |
| **pollution** | *die Verschmutzung* | (dee vairshmootzung) |
| **wind turbine** | *die Windkraftanlage* | (dee vindkraftanlager) |
| **green** | *grün* | (groon) |

One of Europe's biggest wind farms is at Emden in northwest Germany.

## Daily life

German shoppers know they are buying goods in environmentally friendly packaging when they see the "Green Dot." The green dot means that the packaging can either be recycled, or is made from recycled material. The green dot system is now used across Europe.

# Infrastructure: Politics and People

In 1990, Berlin became the capital of a united Germany. The German government meets in the Reichstag. On the front of the building are the words *Dem Deutschen Volke*, which means "For the German people."

The Reichstag in Berlin is where the German government meets.

## YOUNG PEOPLE

The German Youth Parliament began in 1990 and offers young people between the ages of 16 and 22 the opportunity to express their opinions on political and topical issues. Students are encouraged to debate, think independently, and find solutions to problems.

## Political parties

There are two major political parties in the German Bundestag (**parliament**): the Social Democratic Party and the Christian Democratic Union. There are also four smaller parties: the Green Party, the Free Democratic Party, the Christian Social Union, and the Left.

National elections are held every four years, and people age 18 or older can **vote**. The party that gets the most votes wins the most seats in the government. In order to lead, the party with the most votes forms a **coalition** with other parties until they have a **majority**. The **chancellor** is the most powerful minister in the Bundestag, and it is he or she who makes economic, military, and domestic decisions.

## Multicultural, multi-faith

Since the days of the Holy Roman Empire, Germany has always been **multicultural**. The dominant religion is **Christianity**, but there is still a small Jewish population in the country. There is a growing Islamic population, too. A government-sponsored "guest worker" plan in the 1990s attracted many workers from Turkey, and today there are over 200 mosques. The largest mosque is in the city of Cologne.

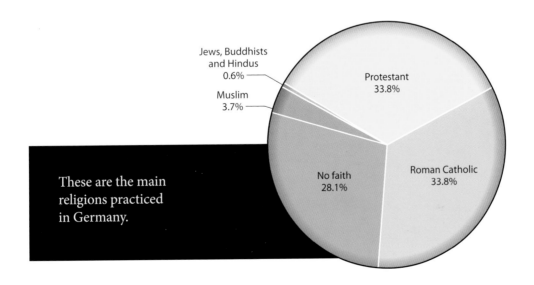

Jews, Buddhists
and Hindus
0.6%

Muslim
3.7%

Protestant
33.8%

No faith
28.1%

Roman Catholic
33.8%

These are the main religions practiced in Germany.

## At school

In Germany education is free in state-run schools. Children have to go to school from the age of 6 up to 15 years old. Before school they attend *Kindergarten*. At primary school, children learn to read and write, as well as study math, history, geography, and science.

### FRIEDRICH FROEBEL (1782–1852)

Friedrich Froebel was born in Oberweissbach, Germany. He created the *Kindergarten* ("children's garden") system that allows children to learn through play. He even designed special toys. In 1851 all *Kindergartens* were closed down because the government thought too much play would make children rebellious! Today *Kindergartens* are established throughout the world.

## High school

There are four types of school that children can go to from the age of ten, depending on what they want to study and how good their grades are. At a *Hauptschule*, students study practical courses, such as plumbing or carpentry. At a *Realschule*, students study subjects like math and languages that will help them get jobs in business. At a *Gymnasium*, students prepare for the *Abitur* exam for entry into a university. This is taken when they are age 19. At a *Gesamtschule*, pupils can study everything, from plumbing and business to subjects like languages and chemistry.

### Daily life

Most German schools start classes at 8 a.m. and finish between 1 p.m. and 2 p.m. Children go home for lunch, and afternoons are usually spent doing homework. Most schools don't have a uniform.

In Germany, a child's first day at school is celebrated with a special gift. A *shultüte* or "school bag" is a decorated paper cone filled with books, pens, pencils, toys, and sweets.

## Health and welfare

When Germans are sick, they go to the doctor. They pay for the **consultation** and claim the costs back on their health **insurance**. The insurance covers the costs of seeing the doctor and of any **prescriptions** or hospital treatment.

Life expectancy for German adults is 79.4 years, which is higher than the United States (78.11) and Britain (79.01), but lower than France (80.98) and Italy (80.2). The World Health Organization (WHO) ranks Germany's health care system as 25th in the world. German people often visit health resorts and spas.

### How to say...

| my ... hurts | mein ... tut mir weh | (mine ... toot meer vey) |
|---|---|---|
| head | das Kopf | (das kopf) |
| arm | der Arm | (dare arm) |
| leg | das Bein | (das byn) |
| stomach | der Bauch | (dare bauk) |
| foot | der Fuß | (dare foos) |
| I have a headache | Ich habe Kopfschmerzen | (ik harba kopfshmarezen) |
| healthy | gesund | (gusoond) |
| ill | krank | (krank) |

### Daily life

The term "spa" means water treatment. Germany has many natural mineral water springs and many spa towns. People go to spas to relax for the day, to drink the healing waters, or to have a course of treatment for an illness, such as arthritis.

## Welfare state

If you can't work, become unemployed, or are retired, social security pays out a living allowance. Employed people pay into state pensions and unemployment insurance plans. Germany spends over 27 percent of its GDP on **welfare**.

Baden-Baden means "baths-baths," and is one of Germany's most famous health spas.

# Culture: Art, Music, and Leisure

Germany's writers, artists, and musicians have influenced culture well beyond Germany's borders. Germany is a country of folklore and myth, with stories of giants in the mountains and mermaids bewitching sailors. It is also a country of writers who re-create the harsh realities of life. Günter Grass and Thomas Mann both won the **Nobel Prize** for literature. Grass' novel *The Tin Drum* is about life in Germany in the early 1900s.

## THE BROTHERS GRIMM

Brothers Jacob (1785–1863) and Wilhelm (1786–1859) Grimm collected folk tales and wrote them down. "The Pied Piper of Hamelin," "Rumplestiltskin," and "Hansel and Gretel" are some of their stories.

## Art world

Germany has a long tradition of both fine art and experimental art. Famous German artist Hans Holbein (1497–1543) was court painter to Henry VIII of England. Albrecht Dürer (1471–1528) became famous for his religious paintings, and Franz Ackermann is a modern **installation artist** and painter, with work exhibited all over the world.

Germany's Rock am Ring and Rock im Park festivals are two of the largest in the world.

## YOUNG PEOPLE

Nearly 200,000 people go to the Rock am Ring and Rock im Park music festivals. They take place every year at the same time in two different places. Artists perform one day at the Ring, a motor racing track, and then one day in the Park in Nuremberg.

## Music maestros

From the great classical composers to the jazz cafés of Potsdam, music is a huge part of German life. The Berlin Philharmonic is considered one of the world's best orchestras, and composers such as Beethoven, Brahms and J. S. Bach are played and listened to everywhere.

## Sport and leisure

Germans love the outdoor life, and many go hiking and camping in the mountains and forests. Skiing, snowboarding, and cross-country skiing are popular winter sports, while bicycling, tennis, and athletics are enjoyed in summer. The largest national sport is soccer, and the *Bundesliga* is the highest league. Germany has won the World Cup three times.

Motorsport is also popular in Germany, with many famous Grand Prix venues, such as the Nürburgring and the Hockenheim race track. The German driver Michael Schumacher won the Formula 1 World Championship a record seven times.

Skiing is a popular sport in the German Alps.

## National holidays

There are nine official public holidays each year in Germany, including Christmas Day. The newest holiday is German Unity Day on October 3. On this day, celebrations are held around the country and at the Brandenburg Gate in Berlin.

## National song

*Deutschlandlied* ("Germany's Song") has been the national anthem since 1922. It is sung on state occasions, before sports matches, and at medal ceremonies.

> *Deutschland, Deutschland über alles,*
> *Über alles in der Welt,*
> *Wenn es stets zu Schutz und Trutze*
> *Brüderlich zusammenhält.*
> *Von der Maas bis an die Memel,*
> *Von der Etsch bis an den Belt,*
> *Deutschland, Deutschland über alles,*
> *Über alles in der Welt!*
>
> *Germany, Germany above all,*
> *Above all in the world,*
> *When, for protection and defense, it always*
> *takes a brotherly stand together.*
> *From the Maas to the Memel,*
> *From the Etsch to the Belt,*
> *Germany, Germany above everything,*
> *Above everything in the world.*

# Food and drink

Germany is a food-loving country, with many food festivals throughout the year. There are over 1,500 varieties of *wurst* (sausage). Other popular foods are *sauerkraut* (pickled cabbage), *schwarzbrot* (rye bread), *apfelstrudel* (apple strudel), and *schwarzwaldkirschtorte* (black forest gateau).

Millions of people attend Munich's famous Oktoberfest beer festival.

## *How to say...*

|  |  |  |
|---|---|---|
| **enjoy your meal** | *guten Appetit* | (gooten appateet) |
| **I would like...** | *Ich möchte...* | (ik murkta) |
| **bread** | *das Brot* | (das broat) |
| **butter** | *die Butter* | (dee booter) |
| **cheese** | *der Käse* | (dare cares-a) |
| **ham** | *der Schinken* | (dare shinken) |
| **sausage** | *die Wurst* | (dee vurst) |
| **beer** | *ein Bier* | (eyn bee-er) |

## Daily life

There are over a thousand breweries across Germany, brewing hundreds of different beers. Beer festivals are common, and Munich's Oktoberfest is the most famous. Each year, more than 6 million people visit the Oktoberfest and drink more than 14 million pints (7 million liters) of beer.

## Lebkuchen (ginger cookies)

Ask an adult to help you make this delicious treat.

### Ingredients

- 2 cups all-purpose flour
- 1 cup ground almonds
- 2 teaspoons ground ginger
- 1 teaspoon ground cinnamon
- 1 teaspoon baking powder
- ⅘ cup (7 oz) clear honey
- ⅓ cup (6 tablespoons) butter
- 1 lemon, finely grated zest
- ¾ cup powdered sugar
- 1 egg white, beaten

### What to do

1. Preheat oven to 350° Fahrenheit (180° Celsius).
2. Put dry ingredients into a large bowl
3. Melt the butter and honey in a pan, then pour into the flour mixture along with the lemon zest. Mix well to make a dough and leave to cool.
4. Roll the dough into about 30 balls, each 1 inch (3 centimeters) wide. Flatten each ball into a round.
5. Place rounds on greased baking trays and bake for 15 minutes.
6. To ice the biscuits, mix together the powdered sugar, egg white, and 1 to 2 tablespoons of water. Dip the top of each cookie in the frosting and leave to dry.

# Germany Today

Tradition and culture are important to German people, and today they enjoy a rich cultural **diversity** and religious freedom. Germany has become an international center for movies, art, and modern technology. Its slick transportation networks and organized town planning give Germans a high standard of living. It is a country that looks to the future while remembering the horrors of the past.

## Thinkers, theorists, and technicians

German philosophers and physicists have considered the meaning of life and the nature of the universe for centuries and have left their mark on global academic study. Thinkers like Goethe and Marx developed social and political theories, while scientists like Einstein and Heisenberg helped to explain the very beginnings of the world.

Today, German scientists and engineers are leading the way in green technologies and sustainable development. German scientists and economists have won 88 Nobel Prizes.

## Worldwide language

You probably use a lot of German words when you speak without even realizing it! If you went to kindergarten, or have eaten a hamburger or frankfurter, or played a glockenspiel, or gotten all dressed up in glitzy clothes, you have used words that have entered the English language from German.

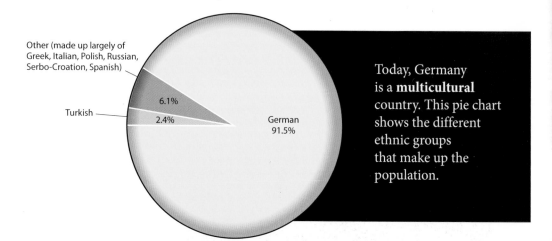

Other (made up largely of Greek, Italian, Polish, Russian, Serbo-Croation, Spanish)

6.1%

Turkish

2.4%

German 91.5%

Today, Germany is a **multicultural** country. This pie chart shows the different ethnic groups that make up the population.

# Making history

Today, multi-ethnic Germany is a forward-looking, prosperous nation that is the vibrant heart of European unity. The huge challenges of balancing wealth and opportunity across the country are being slowly met. In successfully reuniting the old East and West Germany, a united Germany is confidently making its own history as a young nation.

Modern Berlin is a mix of the old and the new, from the modern Unter den Linden to the historic Brandenburg Gate.

# Fact File

| | |
|---|---|
| **Official language:** | German |
| **Capital city:** | Berlin |
| **Bordering countries:** | Poland, Denmark, France, the Netherlands, Belgium, Switzerland, Austria, Luxembourg, Czech Republic |
| **Population:** | over 82 million (74% live in cities) |
| **Largest cities in terms of population:** | Berlin, Hamburg, Munich, Cologne, Frankfurt |
| **Life expectancy:** | 79.4 (male and female average) |
| **WHO health ranking:** | 25th in world |
| **Religion:** | Protestant 33.8%, Roman Catholic 33.8%, Muslim 3.7%, no religion 28.1%, other 0.6% |
| **National symbols:** | black eagle, knapweed (unmarried people wear this in their buttonhole at weddings) |
| **Area:** | 137,846 square miles (357,022 square kilometers) |
| **Land area:** | 134,623 square miles (348,672 square kilometers) |
| **Water area:** | 3,224 square miles (8,350 square kilometers) |
| **Major rivers:** | Rhine 537 miles (865 kilometers) long in Germany, Elbe 452 miles (727 kilometers) long in Germany, Danube 427 miles (687 kilometers) long in Germany |
| **Highest elevation:** | Zugspitze 9,721 feet (2,963 meters) |
| **Currency:** | euro |
| **Natural resources:** | coal, lignite, natural gas, iron ore, copper, nickel, uranium, potash, salt, construction materials, timber, arable land |
| **Imports and exports:** | machinery, vehicles, chemicals, metals, foodstuffs, textiles |
| **Major industries:** | cars and manufacturing—29.7% of workforce involved in manufacturing |

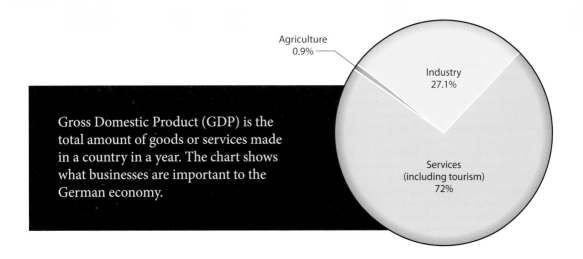

Gross Domestic Product (GDP) is the total amount of goods or services made in a country in a year. The chart shows what businesses are important to the German economy.

Agriculture 0.9%

Industry 27.1%

Services (including tourism) 72%

| | |
|---|---|
| **Literacy rates:** | 99% of the population can read and write |
| **Climate:** | temperate and marine; cool, cloudy, wet winters and summers; occasional warm mountain wind |
| **Units of measurement:** | metric |
| **World Heritage Sites:** | 33 in total, including Aachen cathedral, palaces and parks of Berlin and Potsdam, Zollverein Coal Mine Industrial Complex, Essen |
| **Member of international organizations:** | UN, EU, NATO, G8 |
| **Large German populations elsewhere:** | in the United States there are around 50 million German Americans |
| **Festivals:** | the Oktoberfest beer festival, Berlin Film Festival, Asparagus festival, Darmstadt, Rock am Ring/Rock im Park, Beethoven Festival, Bonn, Potsdam Jazz Festival, Kiel Week sailing festival |
| **Famous Germans:** | Steffi Graf (tennis player), Boris Becker (tennis player), Miroslav Klose (soccer player), Beethoven, Clara Schumann, Bach (composers), Goethe (poet), Albrecht Dürer (artist), Einstein (scientist), Pope Benedict XVI, Levi Strauss (businessman) |

# Timeline

CE is short for Common Era. CE is added after a date and means that the date occurred after the birth of Jesus Christ, for example, 720 CE.

| | |
|---|---|
| 500s CE | Roman rule of Germania |
| 768 CE | Birth of Charlemagne |
| 800 CE | Charlemagne crowned Holy Roman Emperor |
| around 1440 | Johannes Gutenberg invents the printing press |
| 1517 | Martin Luther begins the Reformation by nailing his list of complaints to the cathedral door in Wittenberg |
| 1555 | The Peace of Augsburg allows all German princes to decide the religion of their territories |
| 1648 | The Peace of Westphalia is signed, ending religious wars with Spain and the Netherlands |
| 1685 | Birth of J. S. Bach |
| 1770 | Birth of Beethoven |
| 1782 | Birth of Friedrich Froebel, creator of the *Kindergarten* |
| 1806 | Francis II dissolves the Holy Roman Empire |
| 1812 | The Brothers Grimm publish their first collection of fairy tales |
| 1814–1815 | The Congress of Vienna establishes the German Confederation of 39 independent German states |
| 1819 | Birth of Clara Schumann |
| 1871 | German states unite into one country. Bismarck becomes **Chancellor** of Germany. |
| 1914 | Archduke Franz Ferdinand is assassinated in Sarajevo (now part of Bosnia-Herzegovina), provoking World War I |
| 1918 | End of World War I as Germany is defeated |
| 1919 | The Treaty of Versailles is signed |

| 1921 | Adolf Hitler becomes leader of the National Socialist German Workers Party (Nazi Party) |
| 1922 | Hitler Youth is created. *Deustchlandlied* becomes German national anthem. |
| 1933 | Hitler becomes Chancellor, and Nazi Germany begins persecuting Jews |
| 1936 | Summer Olympic Games in Berlin |
| 1939 | Germany invades Poland, starting World War II |
| 1940 | Germany captures Denmark, Norway, the Netherlands, Belgium, France, and Luxembourg. The Allies, including Russia, Britain, and the United States, retaliate. |
| 1943 | Sophie Scholl and other White Rose Resistance members are executed |
| 1945 | Hitler commits suicide. Germany surrenders and is divided into West and East. Berlin is divided into four zones. |
| 1946 | A pass is required to travel between the different zones in Berlin and Germany |
| 1951 | First International Berlin Film Festival |
| 1954 | West Germany wins the soccer World Cup for the first time |
| 1957 | Leaving East Germany without permission is forbidden |
| 1961 | The Berlin Wall is built. Brandenburg Gate and all other crossing points are closed. |
| 1985 | First Rock am Ring music festival |
| 1989 | The Berlin Wall is demolished, and East Germans are able to travel to the West. The Brandenburg Gate is opened. |
| 1990 | East and West Germany are reunited. October 3 becomes German Unity Day. |
| 2008 | Largest mosque in Germany opens in Cologne. |

# Glossary

**architecture** style of building

**authorities** people in power

**bishopric** historic area governed by a powerful bishop

**chancellor** highest elected position of power in Germany

**Christianity** religion based on the teachings of Christ

**city state** historical city with its own rulers and laws that were valid inside the city walls

**classical** serious, artistic music, often played by an orchestra or piano

**coalition** different political parties working together to govern

**communist** belief in a social system where all people in a country share work and property

**compulsory** required by rules or by law

**concentration camp** prison and death camps where people were sent during World War II

**consultation** discussion or meeting with an expert

**credit crunch** global economic problem caused when the cash flow or credit from banks stops and many businesses cannot get loans. This results in mass unemployment.

**culture** practices, traditions, and beliefs of a society

**democratic** political system where everyone is equal and has the right to vote

**diversity** great variety

**dukedom** area or region ruled by a duke

**economy** to do with money and the industry and jobs in a country

**ecosystem** community of living things

**emissions** gases released into the atmosphere from factories and homes

**euro** currency of some European countries in the EU

**European Union** political and economic union of (currently) 27 European countries

**export** sell goods to another country

**freight** goods transported by road, rail, air, or sea

**G8** group of the eight richest countries in the world

**habitat** environment where a plant or animal is found

**Holy Roman Empire** large empire in Europe that began with the crowning of a German king as Holy Roman Emperor in 962 and is thought to have ended in 1806. The Emperor ruled over various parts of Europe at different times.

**import** buy goods from another country

**installation artist** artist who uses sculpture and other media to create a new sense of space

**insurance** protection

**majority** most people

**multicultural** mix of people from different cultures and countries

**national identity** specific features of a group of people

**Nobel Prize** annual prize awarded to people who have made great advances in science or literature, or have worked toward world peace

**noble** belonging to a high and powerful social class

**parliament** ruling body of a country where laws are made

**prescription** written order for medicine

**Protestant** Christian who practices their faith and doesn't follow the pope's leadership

**Reformation** religious movement started in the 16th century by Martin Luther that resulted in changes in the Protestant church

**renewable energy** power that can be used again, not likely to run out

**resource** means available for a country to develop, such as minerals and energy sources

**Roman Catholic** Christian who follows the beliefs of the Roman Catholic Church and the leadership of the pope

**state** nation or place where people of particular politics or culture are organized into a single group

**stereotype** popular cultural image of something or someone based on very few facts, for example, all Germans like sausages

**sustainable** environmentally friendly

**trade** buying and selling of goods, usually between countries

**tribe** independent social group, historically often made up of primitive or nomadic people

**unemployment** not having a job

**unification** process of joining together

**vote** to choose. People vote for someone to win an election.

**welfare** system of financial assistance for those in need

**World Heritage Site** place of cultural importance that is protected by a United Nations agency

# Find Out More

## Books

De la Bedoyere, Camilla. *Discover Germany*. New York: PowerKids Press, 2010.

Frank, Nicole, and Richard A. Lord. *Germany*. New York: Benchmark Books, 2010.

Hardyman, Robyn. *Germany*. New York: Chelsea House Publications, 2009.

Russell, Henry. *Germany*. Washington, D.C.: National Geographic Children's Books, 2007.

Simmons, Walter. *Germany*. Minneapolis: Bellwether Media, 2010.

## Websites

**http://www.germany.info/Vertretung/usa/en/Startseite.html**
Find plenty of information about Germany on this website.

**https://www.cia.gov/library/publications/the-world-factbook/geos/gm.html**
This CIA World Factbook site has a lot of great information on Germany.

**http://www.cometogermany.com/**
You can find a lot more information about Germany at the National German Tourist Office website.

## Places to visit

If you ever get the chance to go to Germany, here are some of the places you could visit:

**Unten den Linden, Berlin**
Stroll down Berlin's most famous shopping street.

**Brandenburg Gate, Berlin**
Visit the great symbol of a once divided and now united Berlin.

## Berlin Wall, Berlin

There are short sections of the wall still standing around the city, but the longest is the Long East Side Gallery on Mühlenstrasse.

## Reichstag, Berlin

Go up the glass dome and look out over the capital. Go on a tour of the building and sit in on parliament.

## The Jewish Museum, Berlin

www.jmberlin.de/main/EN/homepage-EN.php
Learn about Jewish culture and history, from the earliest European settlements through World War II and into the present day.

## BMW museum, Munich

See how cars have changed over time and try out the interactive displays.

## Rothenburg ob der Tauber

Go back in time when you visit the town's Middle Ages festival. See knights joust and, watch the townsfolk recreate the sights, sounds, and language of 700 years ago.

## Neuschwanstein Castle, Bavaria

Visit King Ludwig II's fantastic mountain-top castle.

## Rhine River cruise

Take a boat trip on the great Rhine River and see the castles, vineyards, and the famous Lorelei Rock.

## Nuremberg Christmas market

Visit the vast Christmas market and try wurst and pickled spargel!

# Topic Tools

You can use these topic tools for your school projects. Trace the map onto a sheet of paper, using the thick black outline to guide you.

The black, red, and gold colors of the German flag are thought to have originally come from the banner of the Holy Roman Emperor (see page 6). This banner showed a black eagle with a red beak and claws on a golden background. Copy the flag design, and then color in your picture. Make sure you use the right colors!

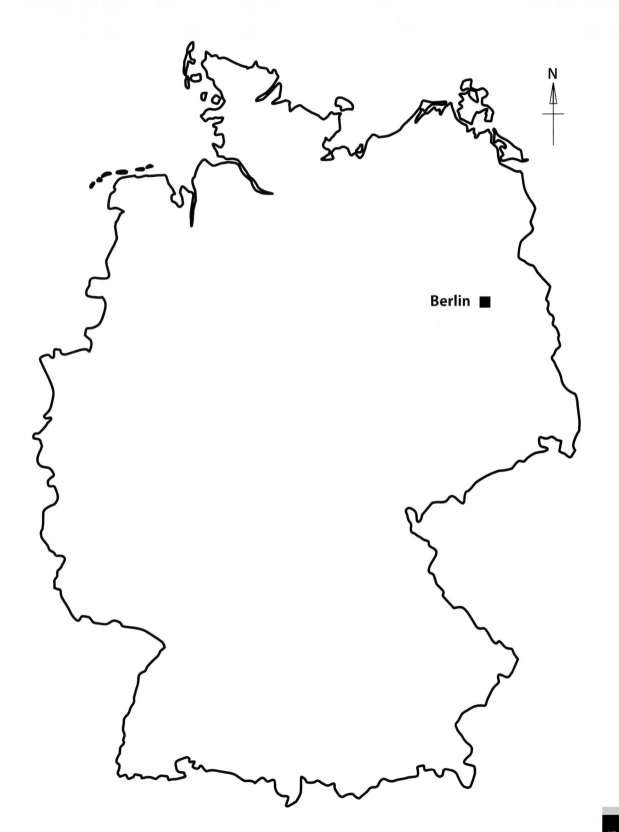

N

**Berlin** ■

# Index

## Titles in the series